Level Three
(C / Grade 2)

Hansel and Gretel

arranged by Wesley Schaum

adapted from the opera by

Engelbert Humperdinck

For Piano Solo

I0804308

Foreword

This classic fairy tale in musical form is based on the well-known story from "Grimm's Fairy Tales." The German composer, Engelbert Humperdinck wrote all of the music himself, but worked with his sister in developing the libretto (story and lyrics). The opera was written in 1891.

Several years earlier, Humperdinck had befriended the well-known opera composer, Richard Wagner. This association with Wagner taught many fine points of orchestration to Humperdick. The music for "Hansel and Gretel" reflects Wagner's influence.

This version has considerable potential for recital use. The narration of the story could be told by the pupil playing the piano or by a second student. A costume recital, with pupils singing the various roles would be appropriate. The entire presentation has many possibilities for music appreciation groups and classrooms.

The pupil gains many sight-reading benefits while learning the pieces in this book. Included are various time signatures, key signatures, tempo marks and accompaniment styles. The grade level is early intermediate.

Incidentally, the composer of this opera bears no relationship to the contemporary popular singer of the same name.

Index

Title	Page
Angels' Descent	11
Brother Come and Dance With Me	4
Children, See the Wonder Wrought	23
Come, Little Mousey	16
Evening Prayer	10
Father's Return	23
Father's Theme (Tra la la la)	6
Hocus, Pocus	17
How Delicious	12
I Am Rosina Dainty Mouth	15
I Shut the Children's Peepers	9
Nibble, Nibble Mousekin	14
Overture	2
Spell Is Broken	22
Susy, Little Susy	3
There Stands a Little Man	8
Witch Is Dead	20
Witch's Dance	18
Witch Within That Wood Doth Dwell	7

SCHAUM PUBLICATIONS, INC.
10235 N. Port Washington Rd. - Mequon, WI 53092

07-50
CO-11

A long time ago, a broom maker and his wife lived in a lonely cottage near the edge of a large forest in the Hartz mountains of Germany. With them lived their son and daughter, Hansel and Gretel.

The whole family helped in making brooms and sharing household chores. It had been several weeks since the father had been able to sell any brooms. They had no money left to buy food and only half a loaf of bread in the cupboard.

OVERTURE

Allegro M.M. ♩=132–152

The next morning everyone had only a small piece of bread for breakfast. The father and mother left the cottage early to again try selling their brooms. Both children had work to do. There were socks for Gretel to mend and several small brooms for Hansel to make. They sang to each other as they worked.

SUSY, LITTLE SUSY

Allegretto M.M. ♩=120–138

With their stomachs nearly empty it was difficult for them to concentrate on their work. After a while Gretel urged Hansel to put down his broom and dance with her.

BROTHER COME AND DANCE WITH ME

Just as they were having the most fun, their mother suddenly entered the room. She scolded them for dancing and playing when there was work to be done. Angrily she gave Hansel and Gretel a basket and sent them into the forest to gather strawberries for supper. Soon the children wandered out of sight.

During the day the father had been very lucky and was able to sell all of his brooms at a good price in a nearby town. It was late as he returned home carrying large bags of groceries. As he approached the cottage he sang happily.

FATHER'S THEME

Eagerly the mother and father unpacked the food and started to prepare supper, but the children had not returned from the woods. The father was afraid they may have become lost and captured by a witch who lived in the forest. The mother and father then rushed out to search for Hansel and Gretel.

A WITCH WITHIN THAT WOOD DOTH DWELL

In the meantime, the children had wandered far into the woods looking for strawberries. They were so hungry that they ate most of what they picked. Gretel sang to herself along the way.

THERE STANDS A LITTLE MAN

The words for this piece are really a riddle. The answer is shown in the picture on this page.

As darkness approached, Hansel realized that he had lost the way. They both became frightened as they heard strange noises in the forest. However, the sandman's approach soothed their fears and made the children drowsy.

I SHUT THE CHILDREN'S PEEPERS

Before lying down to sleep on a pile of soft leaves they say their customary evening prayer.

EVENING PRAYER

As they sleep they dream about their guardian angels who visit them.

ANGEL'S DESCENT

Tranquillo M.M. ♩=69–80

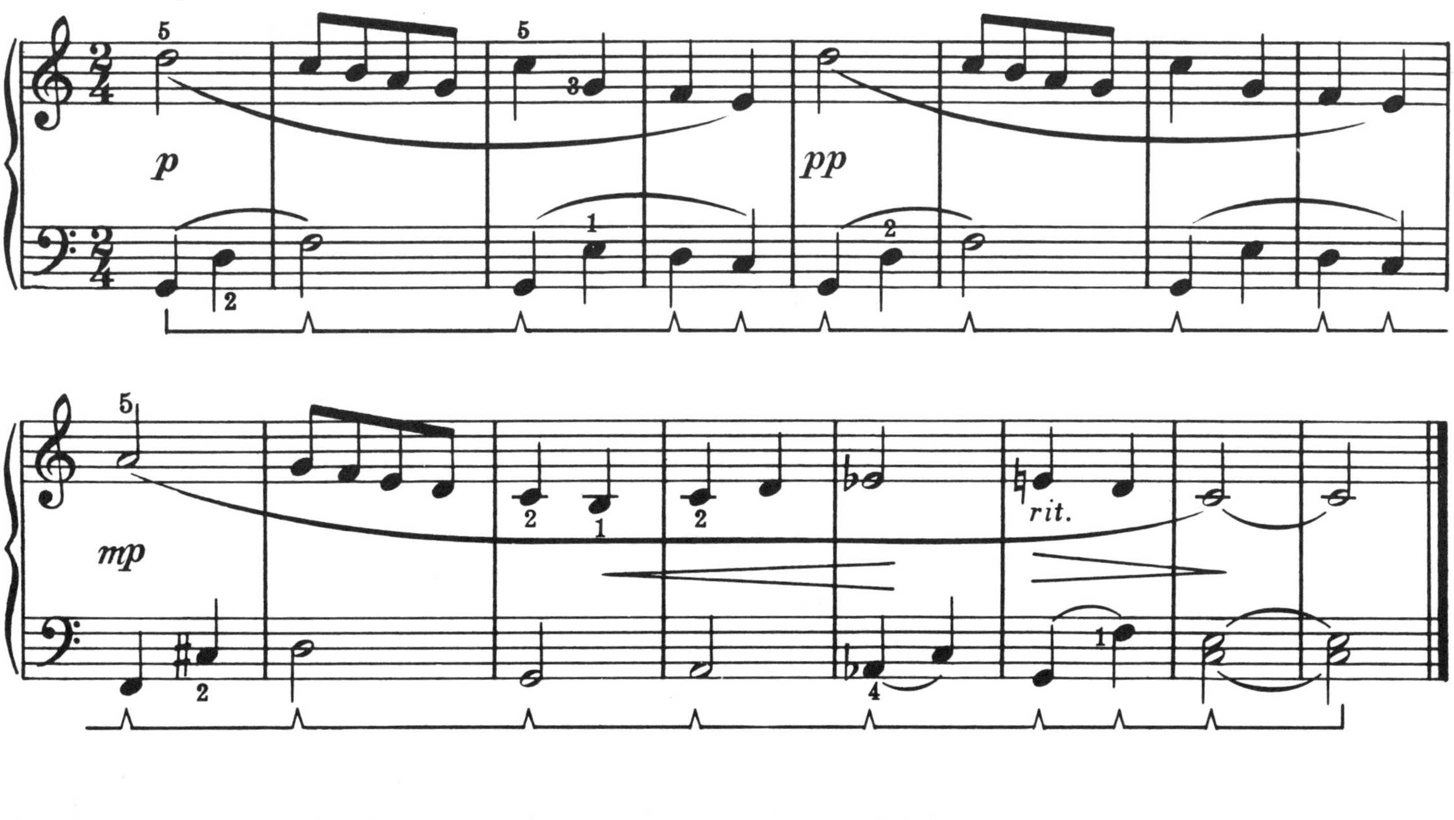

As the morning mist clears, Hansel and Gretel see that they are very near a fascinating looking house made of cakes and cookies and decorated with all kinds of candy and goodies.

HOW DELICIOUS

Giocoso M.M. ♩=132–160

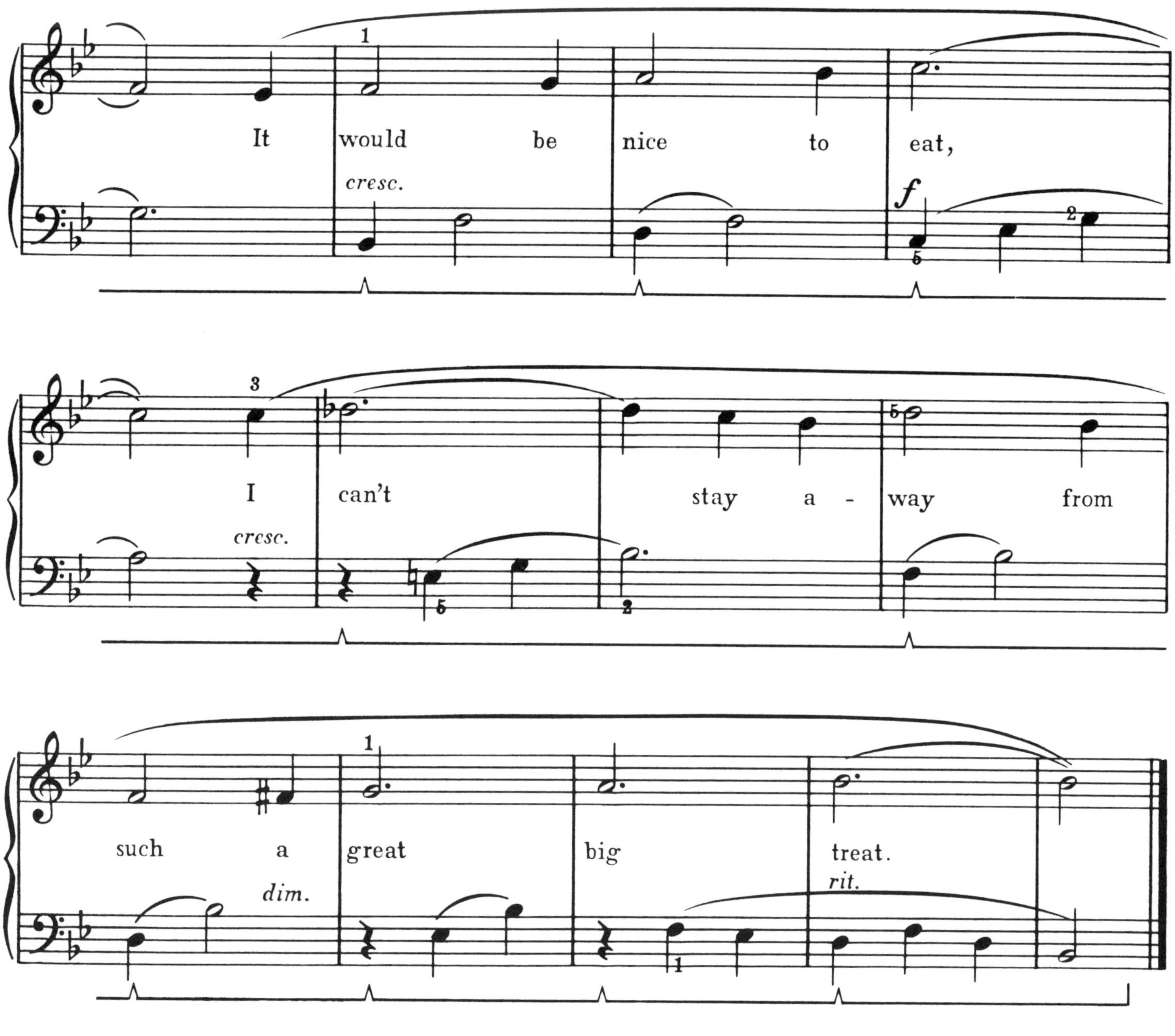
It would be nice to eat,
cresc.
f
I can't stay a - way from
cresc.
such a great big treat.
dim.
rit.

The house is so tempting that the children run up and begin to break away small pieces to taste them. They do not realize that this is really the house of the witch whose voice can be heard from inside.

NIBBLE, NIBBLE MOUSEKIN

Leggiero M. M. ♩=54–63

Hansel and Gretel are both so busy eating that they pay no attention to the voice until the witch comes outside and introduces herself.

I AM ROSINA DAINTY MOUTH

Andantino M.M. ♩. = 48–54

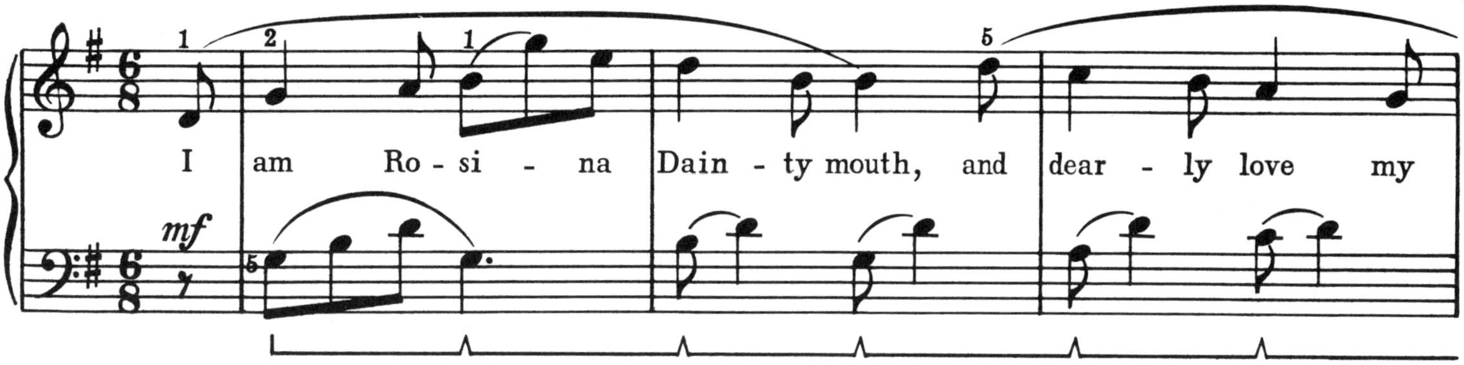

The witch is very ugly and awkward and the children are afraid. The witch tries to persuade them to come into the house.

COME, LITTLE MOUSEY

Allegro M.M. ♩=132–152

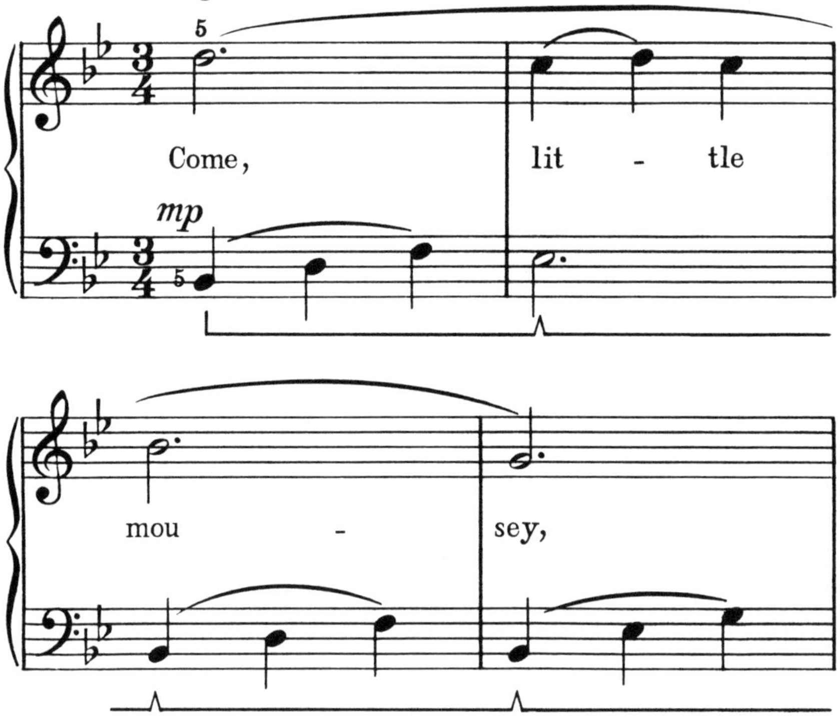

Hansel and Gretel back away but the witch casts a spell on them so they cannot move.

HOCUS, POCUS

Misterioso M.M. ♩=44–50

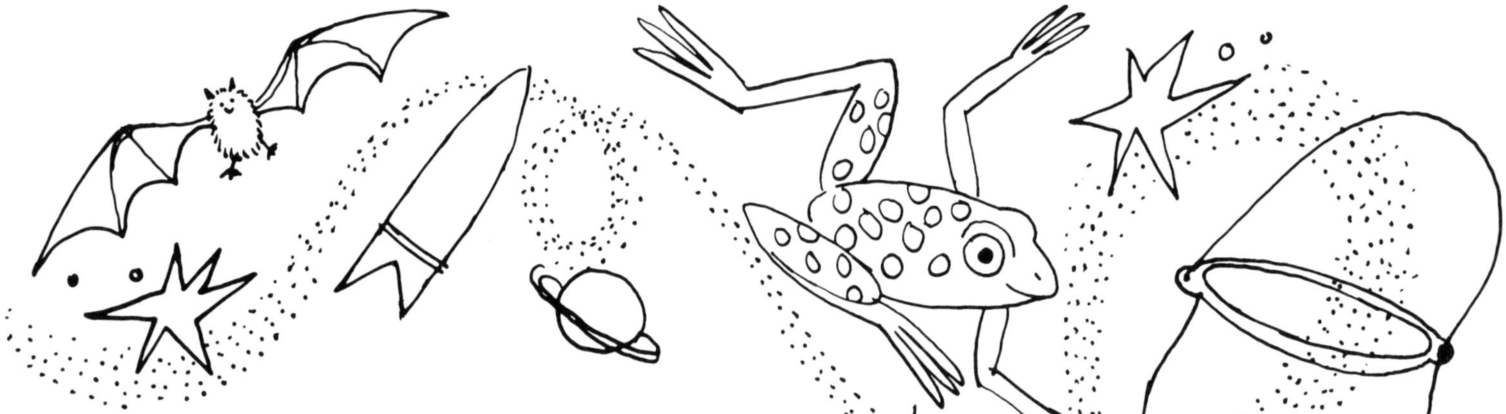

The witch plans to lure the children into her magic oven and bake them both into gingerbread, the witch's favorite food. Gleefully the witch celebrates her latest capture by riding on her broomstick.

WITCH'S DANCE

Agitato M.M. ♩=132–160

five and six are witch-es' tricks, And
nine is one, and ten is none, And sev'n is nil, Or what she will! So
hop, hop, hop, gal-lop, lop, lop, My broom-stick nag, don't lag.

After her wild ride, the witch returns and recites magic words which break the spell on Gretel. The witch hopes to lure the girl into the oven.

Gretel is suspicious of the witch and pretends not to understand. When the witch's back is turned, Gretel repeats the magic words to break the spell on Hansel.

As the witch tries to coax Gretel into the oven, Gretel again pretends not to understand. The impatient witch demonstrates to Gretel how to open the oven door and look inside. As the witch is bent over in front of the open oven, both children give a great shove, pushing her into the oven and quickly close the door behind her. The witch screams inside the hot oven and is soon consumed by the flames.

THE WITCH IS DEAD

Animato M.M. ♩=132–152

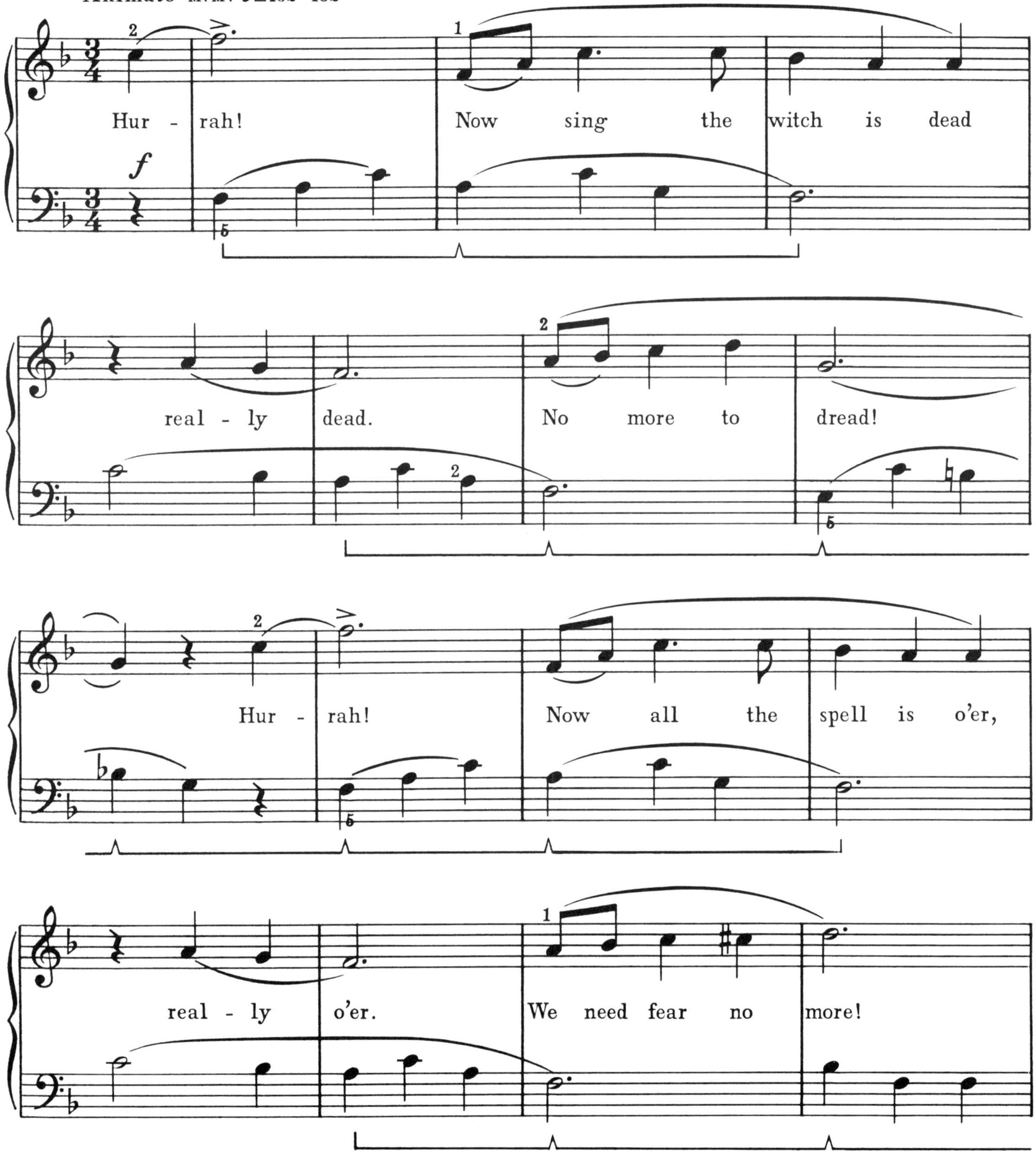

Oh let us hap - py be, dan - cing so mer - ri - ly.
Now the old witch is gone, We'll have some fun.
1
2

As the witch dies, the oven explodes. This breaks the spell on dozens of other children transformed into gingerbread figures around the witch's house. They all join in a celebration.

THE SPELL IS BROKEN

Vivace M.M. ♩=138–160

In the meantime, Hansel and Gretel's parents have been searching the forest all thru the night. The father's voice is heard as he approaches.

FATHER'S RETURN

Vivo M.M. ♩=116–132

Mother, father and children are now happily reunited.

CHILDREN, SEE THE WONDER WROUGHT

Con moto M.M. ♩=120–138

Successful Schaum Sheet Music

This is a Partial List — Showing Level 3 and selected Level 4

• = Original Form   * = Big Notes   ✓ = Chord Symbols

LEVEL

AMERICAN – PATRIOTIC SOLOS
58-30 ✓ANCHORS AWEIGH ... *Zimmerman* ... 3
61-35 ✓BATTLE HYMN of the REPUBLIC ... *Steffe* ... 4
58-44 ✓CAISSONS SONG (U.S. Field Artillery) ... 3
58-21 ✓DIXIE ... *Emmett* ... 3
58-45 ✓SEMPER FIDELIS (U.S. Marines) ... *Sousa* ... 3
61-36 ✓STARS and STRIPES FOREVER ... *Sousa* ... 4
58-18 ✓STAR-SPANGLED BANNER . *Commemorative Ed.* ... 3
61-13 YANKEE DOODLE ... *Theme & Variations* ... 4
58-10 ✓YOU'RE A GRAND OLD FLAG ... *Cohan* ... 3

ANIMALS and BIRDS
58-56 • BUCKING BRONCO (L.H. Melody) ... *King* ... 3
61-38 • FROG IN THE FOG (L.H. Melody) ... *Endres* ... 4

BOOGIE
58-25 • BAGPIPE BOOGIE (Grace Notes) ... *Leach* ... 3
58-05 • BEACH BALL BOOGIE ... *Schaum* ... 4

CHRISTMAS
81-02 ✓LET IT SNOW! LET IT SNOW! ... *Styne* ... 3
70-06 ✓SANTA'S ON HIS WAY ... *Schaum* ... 4

CIRCUS
58-42 • GREASE PAINT GERTIE ... *McKinley* ... 3

CLASSICS
61-41 AVE VERUM ... *Mozart* ... 4
61-42 FIRST SYMPHONY THEME (4th Mvt) ... *Brahms* ... 4
58-24 * JOY PRELUDE ("Jesu Joy of Man's Desiring") . *Bach* ... 3
61-09 MINUET MEDLEY (G Major - G Minor) ... *Bach* ... 4
61-14 BEETHOVEN'S 5th SYMPHONY (1st Mvt. Theme) ... 4
58-39 BEETHOVEN'S 7th SYMPHONY (2nd Mvt. Theme) ... 3
61-02 FUR ELISE ... *Beethoven* ... 4
61-11 SONATA IN C (Both Hands in Treble) ... *Mozart* ... 4
58-15 SYMPHONY No. 40 (First Theme) ... *Mozart* ... 3
61-46 TALES FROM THE VIENNA WOODS ... *Strauss* ... 4
61-45 TRUMPET CONCERTO THEME ... *Haydn* ... 4
61-08 TURKISH MARCH ("Rondo alla Turka") ... *Mozart* ... 4
61-30 DANCE OF THE HOURS ... *Ponchielli* ... 4
58-34 MINUET IN D ... *Salieri* ... 3
61-34 WATER MUSIC (Bouree) ... *Handel* ... 3

COUNTRY/WESTERN
58-38 AMERICAN INDIAN SUITE ... *4 Tribal Themes* ... 3
58-33*✓YELLOW ROSE, The ... *Traditional* ... 3

DESCRIPTIVE MUSIC
61-49 • ALMOST BAROQUE ... *Revezoulis* ... 4
61-48 • APPALACHIAN SUNRISE ... *Schwabe* ... 4
61-37 • BAREFOOT FROLIC ... *Cahn* ... 4
58-48 • COUNTY FAIR ... *Leach* ... 3
61-43 • MORNING'S PROMISE ... *Cahn* ... 4
58-53 • PERPETUAL MOTION (6/8 Time) ... *Cahn* ... 3
58-47 • SLEEPY ALARM CLOCK ... *Cahn* ... 3

DUETS (1 Piano, 4 Hands)
71-03 BIRTHDAY BOUQUET ... *Theme & Variations* ... 4
71-01 ENTERTAINER ... *Joplin* ... 4
71-08 • OOM-PAH-PAH (Solo and Duet) ... *Cahn* ... 3

ETHNIC MUSIC
58-07 ✓HAVA NAGILA (Minor Key) ... *Israeli Folk Dance* ... 3
61-24 TARANTELLA (6/8 Time) ... *Italian Folk Dance* ... 4

LEVEL

HALLOWEEN
61-05 FUNERAL MARCH of a MARIONETTE ... *Gounod* ... 4
58-41• GHOSTLY JIVE (Minor Key) ... *Leach* ... 3

JAZZ
58-19 • COUNTRY ROCK ... *Jones* ... 3
61-18 • HAPPY TRUMPET ... *Muniz* ... 4
80-08 ✓IN THE MOOD ... *Garland* ... 3
61-34 • MIZ TUTTLE SHUFFLE ... *Leach* ... 4
58-57 • RUNAROUND ROCK ... *Biel* ... 3

MARCHES
61-04 • CARAVAN (6/8 Time) ... *Kahl* ... 4
58-50 ✓WASHINGTON POST MARCH ... *Sousa* ... 3

MINOR KEY
58-43 *•DRIZZLY DAY (Minor Key) ... *Holmes* ... 3
61-26 ✓SCARBOROUGH FAIR ... *English Folk Song* ... 4
58-49 • SUMMER SCHERZO ... *Leach* ... 3

MOVIE THEMES
80-02 OVER THE RAINBOW (from "Wizard of Oz") *Arlen* ... 3

OLDIES but GOODIES
58-02 ✓GIVE MY REGARDS TO BROADWAY ... *Cohan* ... 3

RAGTIME
61-33 • BABY BRONTOSAURUS RAG ... *McKinley* ... 4
61-10 ✓ENTERTAINER ... *Joplin* ... 4
58-51• RAMBLIN' RAG ... *King* ... 3

ROMANTIC MOOD
58-31 ASPIRATION ... *Schumann* ... 3
58-01 ✓FASCINATION WALTZ ... *Marchetti* ... 3
61-40 INTERMEZZO IN D ... *Sor* ... 4
58-36 ✓LET ME CALL YOU SWEETHEART ... *Friedman* ... 3
61-03 MELODY IN F (2/4 Time) ... *Rubinstein* ... 4

SACRED
61-17 DONA NOBIS PACEM ("Grant Us Thy Peace") ... 4
58-32 ✓JUST A CLOSER WALK WITH THEE ... *Spiritual* ... 3

SHOW TUNES
80-21 ✓SEND IN THE CLOWNS ... *Sondheim* ... 3

SHOWY DISPLAY SOLOS
61-06 BIRTHDAY BOUQUET ... *Theme & Variations* ... 4
61-39 • HORSIN' AROUND ... *Weston* ... 4

6/8 TIME
61-50 • TWILIGHT BELLS ... *King* ... 4

SPORTS
58-23 • SKATEBOARD (Cross Hands) ... *Schaum* ... 3

SPRINGTIME
58-52 • APRIL WALK ... *Levin* ... 3
61-47 • FLOATING IN THE CLOUDS ... *Nica* ... 4

STACCATO
58-55 • TANGO PIZZICATO ... *Cahn* ... 3

SYNCOPATION
58-54 • SOMBRERO ... *Cahn* ... 3